BERMUDA: ISLAND PORTRAIT

Dave Saunders

GIS Bermuda

CARIBBEAN

To my father, who set a good example

First published 1999 by
MACMILLAN EDUCATION LTD
London and Basingstoke
Companies and representatives throughout the world

ISBN 0–333–73701–6

10   9   8   7   6   5   4   3   2   1
07   06   05   04   03   02   01   00   99   98

This book is printed on paper suitable for recycling and made from fully managed and
sustained forest sources.

Typeset by *T* Tek Art, Croydon, Surrey
Printed in Hong Kong

A catalogue record for this book is available from the British Library

All photographs by Dave Saunders except pp iii and 118
Cover design by Stafford and Stafford.
Front cover: Horseshoe Bay beach, Southampton.
Spine: Grace Methodist Church.
Half title page: Early morning at Cambridge Beaches, Sandys.
Title page: Bermuda viewed from the east, with the airport and St David's Head in
the foreground.
Page v: Bird of paradise flower (*Strelitzia reginae*) in the Botanical Gardens.
Back cover: Bermuda Regimental band marches past the Cabinet Building, Hamilton.

CONTENTS

BERMUDA

Fort St Catherine

Tobacco Bay

ST GEORGE'S

Mullet Bay

Whale Bone Bay

Airport

ST GEORGE'S

St David's Head

Royal Naval Dockyard

The Causeway

HAMILTON

Castle Harbour

Daniel's Head

Mangrove Bay

Harrington Sound

Flatts Inlet

TUCKER'S TOWN

Spanish Point

SANDYS

PEMBROKE

DEVONSHIRE

SMITH'S

Great Sound

Ely's Harbour

HAMILTON

Somerset Bridge

PAGET

A T L A N T I C
O C E A N

SOUTHAMPTON

WARWICK

Gibb's Hill

Horseshoe Bay

N

QUO·FATA·FERUNT

It's easy to love Bermuda. Those who visit for a day or two immediately sense its charm. Those who stay a week or more invariably yearn to return. And those who live here know that this is the nearest place to paradise on earth.

But it was not always so. And it's worth dipping into the island's history to appreciate how Bermuda arrived at its present privileged position.

Until the early seventeenth century all reports of the islands evoked fear and suspicion. Treacherous fringing reefs wrecked many a ship and earned the name 'Isles of Devils'. Then Admiral Sir George Somers, on his way from Plymouth, England to Jamestown, Virginia, was grounded off the east coast of Bermuda in 1609 and discovered a surprisingly hospitable land. He found a larder full of tasty fish and wild hogs, a plentiful supply of cedar trees for building, and a congenial climate.

The British soon realised that Bermuda could be very useful and, in 1612, dispatched over 50 colonists who established a settlement in St George's.

Ever since Somers forged a link between Bermuda and Virginia, the population's affinities have been shared between the UK and the USA. Political alliance may have been to the English crown, but strategic and economic circumstances often created closer ties with the USA. After all, London is some 3,450 miles away to the east, and New York just 750 miles to the north.

In 1775, when the American colonies rebelled against Britain, supporters of George Washington secretly rolled 100 kegs of gunpowder from St George's onto an American frigate bound for Boston. Nearly a century later, during the American Civil War, Bermuda provided an ideal transshipment point for highly lucrative blockade-running. Fast, slim vessels shuttled between Bermuda and the southern ports, exchanging guns and ammunition for cotton which then fetched high prices in England.

The twentieth century saw much greater co-operation between the UK and USA. During

World War II the USA developed military bases in Southampton Parish and on St David's Island, which included reclaiming land and building a new airport. Then, after over 50 years, on 1st September 1995, the 1,330 acres of military land was handed back to the Bermuda government – some 10 per cent of the country's total land mass.

With a total area of just over 20 square miles, Bermuda is smaller than Manhattan or the Channel island of Guernsey. On this long, curving archipelago of over 150 islands you are always less than one mile from the ocean. This coral cap perched on top of an extinct submarine volcano is one of the most isolated populated countries. Yet Bermuda is one of the biggest little islands in the world. Its small size helps make Bermuda more manageable both for visitors and for those guiding the country's phenomenal success. Bermuda has the atmosphere and population of a small town, yet the aspirations and achievements of an international player. Although its seven principal, connected islands total little more than 20 miles in length and less than two miles in width, Bermuda has become an economic force of international stature.

After varying success with tobacco growing, whaling, pirating, salt trading and onion farming, Bermuda discovered tourism. Or vice versa. Queen Victoria's daughter, Princess Louise, wife of Canada's Governor General, came to Bermuda in 1883 to escape Canada's winter. The following year the island's first resort opened – the Princess Hotel. By 1908, 5,400 tourists a year were following the princess's example. The Royal Gazette called for investors to build more hotels, and advocated encouraging visitors "of the most desirable class only." Today the number of visitors has risen to over half a million a year and there are plenty of prestigious resorts to pamper them.

Since 1992 international business has outstripped tourism as a revenue earner. Based on the infrastructure provided by tourism – good air services, accommodation, service and communications – combined with the tax, regulatory and legislative advantages, blue chip companies have thrived here.

Bermuda is a country renowned for its British reserve and dignified informality. Although some of the formality is relaxing, visitors are expected to conform to certain carefully cultivated conventions concerning clothing and conduct.

On 16th August 1995, having toyed with the prospect of its own independence from Britain, Bermuda voted overwhelmingly in favour of the security and stability of remaining an internally self-governing British dependency.

Bermudians enjoy a comfortable confidence. An easy affability. A genteel efficiency. Like a swan, everything appears serene, civilised, respectable, yet there's a lot of paddling beneath the surface to keep it on course.

Bermuda is special. And taking photographs of the island is invariably satisfying. Stand almost anywhere and look around you. Point the camera and shoot. Your batting average is sure to be high, given the photogenic subjects that present themselves around every corner. The misty mornings and fiery sunsets. The vibrant blooms and tranquil coves. The well-kept churches and well-loved homes. The softly-spoken smiles and crisp regimental regalia. The history and the mystery. The adventure and the elegance.

Bermuda is virtually free from pollution, poverty and the more dowdy signs of commercialism. After nearly 400 years of human habitation, this pastel pattern of islands has emerged beautiful, prosperous and welcoming.

A well-loved island. And rightly so.

Dave Saunders, 1998

Hamilton sits on a sheltered harbour. Only the
cathedral and City Hall stand out on the skyline.
In 1815 the capital was transferred from
St George's to Hamilton.

HAMILTON AND PEMBROKE

Johnny Barnes has become something of a personality. Every weekday morning since 1974 between 5 and 10 am at the roundabout just outside the city, he has been greeting commuters with the words "I love you; you're beautiful."

The City Hall, opened in 1960, houses an art gallery, exhibition hall and theatre. The weathervane on top of the tower is in the shape of the sailing ship *Sea Venture*, wrecked off the east coast in 1609.

Lifelike sculptures by Desmond Fountain are found
throughout the island in appropriate and often
unexpected locations.

Sessions House is the home of the Parliamentary
Assembly and Supreme Court.

Front Street presents an architectural medley of
decorated facades and ornate balconies, behind
which wait imported, tax-free goods from Britain,
Europe and America.

Cedar Bridge Academy. Education is free and compulsory for
children from five to 16. Bermuda's literacy rate is 98 per cent.
The curriculum draws on systems from both the USA and UK.

A Bermuda dinghy is suspended in the atrium of the ACE Building on Par La Ville Road. ACE is one of Bermuda's largest companies specialising in insurance and reinsurance for the international market.

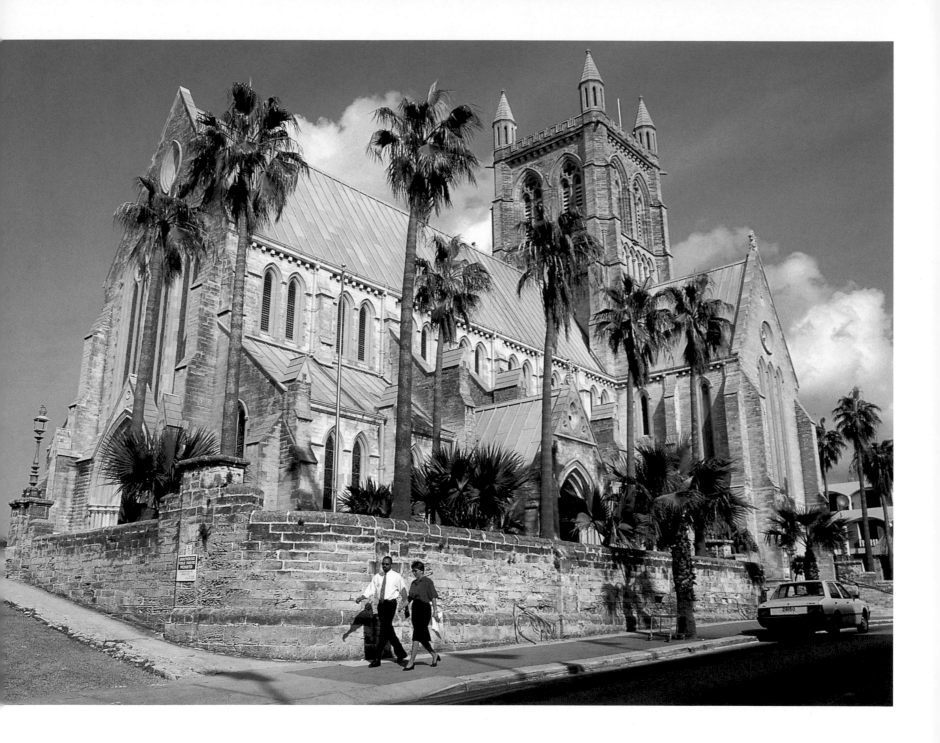

Horse-drawn carriages are a common sight on Front Street.

(Left) The Anglican Cathedral, consecrated in 1911, echoes the style of early English cathedrals.

A horse-drawn carriage adds a touch of style to
a wedding party.

Traditionally honeymooners walk through a circular limestone moongate and make a wish.

Restrictions on car ownership and the absence of car rentals has given rise to over 22,000 motorbikes and scooters around the island – more than the number of cars. Many drivers find it difficult to keep to the official speed limit of 35 kph (22 mph).

Some 30 per cent of the annual half a million tourists arrive by cruise ship during the summer months. Only four cruise ships are permitted in Bermuda at a time.

Bermuda has been called a floating golf course. There are more golf courses per square mile than anywhere in the world . . .
and they all have breath-taking views over the Atlantic coastline.

Teeing off at Castle Harbour's 18-hole golf course.
Several hotels have golf courses on their own grounds.
Castle Harbour Hotel, opened in 1931, occupies
260 acres – the largest privately-owned property in
Bermuda. Its golf course is 6,445 yards, par 71.

Harness racing at the National Equestrian Centre. (*and previous pages*)

Horse riding beside St Mark's Church, Smith's.

The Tornado World Championship is a 10-race
event attracting over 70 crews, drawn to
Bermuda's fair winds.

St George's is one of many mooring sites for
the yachting fraternity.

The Dog Shows held in March and November draw contestants from the USA and Canada, as well as Bermuda's best.

The Bermuda rugby team battles it out against the force of the visiting South Africans in the World Rugby Classic at the National Sports Club.

Along with cricket, soccer attracts an enthusiastic following. Local teams – Boulevard and Vasco de Gama – compete in the final.

The next generation of players.

Soccer spectators at the National

Sports Centre.

Supporters of the winning team
display their colours.

That victorious feeling.
Boulevard win the cup.

Gombey dancers traditionally perform on Boxing Day and New Year's Day. In grotesque masks and colourful costumes adapted from American Indians, they dance to West African tribal rhythms.

Newstead Hotel, Paget, is a quiet, elegant manor house.

The pool at Newstead overlooks the harbour and Hamilton, just a short ferry ride away.

The tidal flow is intensified as water rushes under Flatts Bridge – Harrington Sound's only obvious link to the ocean at Flatts Inlet.

Flatts Inlet provides a sheltered haven for boats.

Over-fishing has depleted stocks in the waters surrounding the island such that little commercial fishing takes place, yet small scale sport fishing still thrives.

Flatts Inlet.

Bermuda boasts the northernmost coral reefs in the Atlantic – thanks to the warm currents of the Gulf Stream. The Aquarium, Museum and Zoo in Flatts village displays over 100 species of tropical and subtropical fish and 48 species of hard and soft corals found around the island.

Scooters provide the most versatile mode of transport for tourists.

Oleander (*Nerium oleander*) hedges fringe many of the roads,
especially on the more sheltered south side of the island.
Shrubs grow up to 20 feet tall.

Harrington Sound Road.

Trees have played a key role in Bermuda's development. Originally three endemic trees covered much of the island – the Bermuda cedar, palmetto and Bermuda olivewood. They have provided the raw material for the building of ships, houses and furniture. Some 90 per cent of the native cedars were devastated by blight in the 1940s. Today these have been largely replaced by fast-growing casuarina or whistling pine.

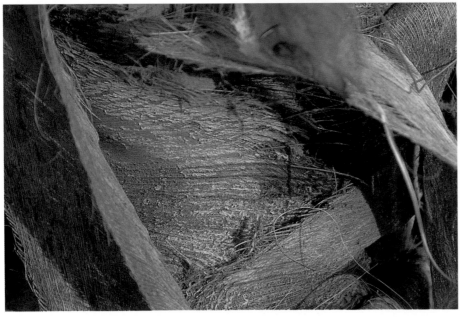

(Right) Red is the most common colour of hibiscus (*Hibiscus rosa sinensis*), though they also come in white, yellow or orange.

Some of the best examples of the bird of paradise flower (*Strelitzia reginae*) can be found at the Botanical Gardens, Devonshire. The crest of the 'bird' comprises up to six flowers that lift out of the sheath. Each flower has three pointed orange petals with blue stamens shaped like arrowheads. They are related to the banana and are native of South Africa.

This ground-hugging cycad grows in the garden of the National Trust's eighteenth century Verdmont Museum in Smith's Parish. Feathery, evergreen leaves radiate from a seed-bearing dome, giving it a palm-like appearance. Cycads are called living fossils because they have changed little in 100 million years.

The honeycup, chalice cup vine or golden chalice (*Solandra maxima*) blooms in late summer for four days, climbing up or tumbling over other vegetation, walls and fences. It is a member of the potato family and native of Mexico and tropical America.

Morning glory, bluebell or blue dawn flower (*Ipomoea indica*) grows
prolifically at up to one foot a day during the growing season.
Hibiscus (*Hibiscus rosa sinensis*) blooms almost continually
throughout the year.

The torch plant or candelabra aloe (*Aloe arborescens*) grows island-wide.

The red stamens of the weeping bottle brush tree (*Callistemon viminalis*) droop gracefully like the weeping willow. It belongs to the Myrtle family from Australia. When the fruits are hard and dry they look like small grey buttons.

There are over 300 edible forms of banana (*Musa acuminata*). Each tree produces only one stem of bananas. The plant dies when it has fruited, but a new one grows from its base.

Indigenous to the Caribbean and Central America, the pawpaw or papaya (*Carica papaya*) begins to bear fruit after one year, and can be eaten green as a vegetable or when ripe yellow as a fruit. Pawpaw sap contains papain, a digestive enzyme used as a meat tenderizer.

Rocky cove and cliffs to the west of
Horseshoe Bay, Southampton.

Horseshoe Bay is a quarter of a mile crescent of powdery white sand bounded by rocky outcrops.

Dolphins interact with visitors at Dolphin Quest near the
Southampton Princess beach club.

Like whales, dolphins are cetaceans – marine
mammals that breathe air. Dolphins use sonar
and magnetism for navigation. They are
intelligent and seem to enjoy
contact with humans.

Gibb's Hill Lighthouse is perched on the 245 ft Gibb's Hill. It was erected in 1846 and, at nearly 120 ft tall, is the tallest cast-iron lighthouse in the world. There is a clear 360 degree panorama for those who climb the 185 steps.

'Christopher' – sculpture by Desmond
Fountain waits outside the Southampton
Princess Hotel, Bermuda's biggest resort
complex, opened in 1972.

Gibb's Hill Lighthouse overlooks the
Southampton Princess 18-hole, par
three golf course.

Elbow Beach Hotel pool and quarter of a mile beach fringe the 29 acre property which comprises both a hotel and a cottage colony.

Shutters keep out the direct glare of the sun, while allowing a flow of air through the house. The picturesque pink and blue building in Mullet Bay is one of the island's most photographed houses.

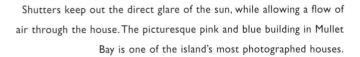

Ornate gables and pastel hues typify Bermudian houses.

'Cake icing' stepped rooves are lime-washed regularly to purify rainwater that is channelled into tanks for household use. Bermuda has no rivers or lakes, but over 50 inches of rainfall a year.

St Anne's Parish Church, Southampton. Most Bermudians are Christians, with Anglicans being the largest denomination.

St John The Evangelist Church, Pembroke.

Grace Methodist Church.

St Peter's Church on St George's Island is the oldest Anglican church
in continuous use in the western hemisphere.

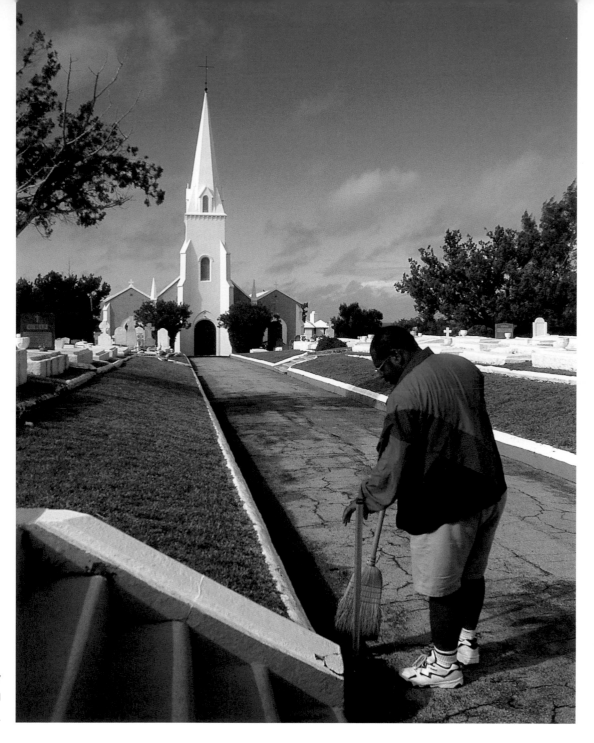

St James' Church in Sandys is an eighteenth century parish church, damaged by hurricanes on several occasions and repeatedly rebuilt.

In the grounds of a nineteenth century house on Middle Road is an old buttery – a small square outbuilding with a steep pyramidal roof and thick walls of Bermuda limestone, once used to keep food cool.

The wide verandahs of old Bermudian homes provide comfortable, shaded places to sit.

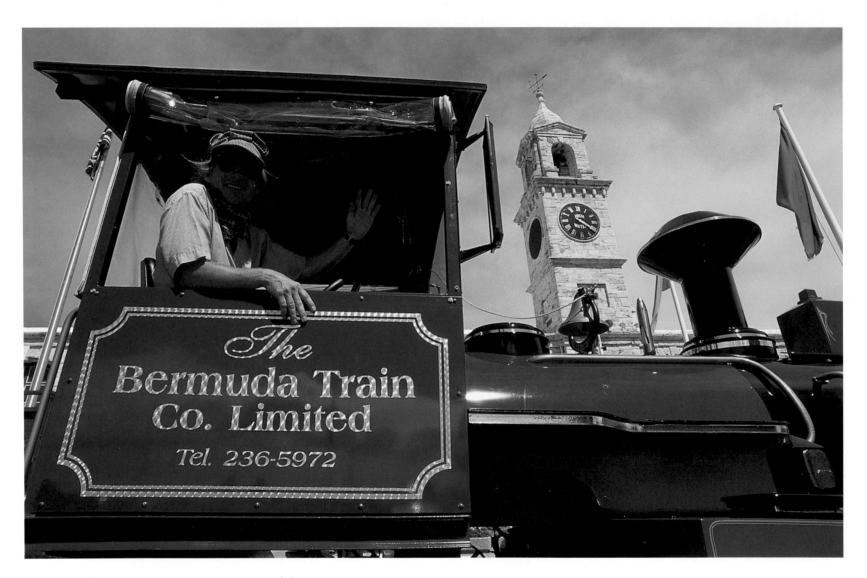

The Bermuda Train Company transports visitors around the
imaginatively renovated Royal Naval Dockyard.

The East Storehouse of the Dockyard is dominated by twin 100 ft stone towers. Built by the British on Ireland Island in 1810, it now features a collection of shops and bars.

Somerset Bridge is the world's smallest drawbridge, leaving
less than 2 ft to slide a yacht's mast through.

The Maritime Museum, once the keep of the Royal Naval Dockyard, where munitions were stored, is Bermuda's biggest and best museum. It houses exhibits of boats, wrecks, old currency and Bermuda's history of diving and whaling. In the Boatloft, the Bermuda pilot gig *Rambler* last used in 1929, is on show. Six or eight oarsmen used to rush a pilot out to arriving ships.

Looking across the mouth of Great Sound from

Spanish Point.

Sitting unobtrusively on a bench outside reception at Cambridge Beaches is another of Desmond Fountain's sculptures.

Founded in 1920, Cambridge Beaches first developed the cottage colony concept, involving a scatter of apartments around a dining room, bar and pool.

Looking across Somerset Long Bay to Daniel's Head, Sandys.

Sunset at the Scaur, Sandys.

West End

(Right and far right) Mangrove Bay, Sandys.

War veteran in St George's on Remembrance Day.

Friends discuss past times in St George's. About three quarters of all islanders were born in Bermuda.

Stevie Dread outside his shop – Abyssinia Imports – on
Court Street in Hamilton.

A soldier of the Bermuda Regiment waits in front of the Cenotaph in Hamilton on the occasion of the opening of Parliament.

Johnny Barnes welcomes everyone.

Wigs and gowns are worn by Supreme Court judges and
lawyers on formal occasions – this time for the signing in
of the new Governor.

Hamilton Fire Station on King Street conducts
regular practice drills.

Not all the police in Bermuda wear
British-style helmets.

National parks were first established in Bermuda in 1986 to protect environmentally sensitive areas. Park rangers now oversee dozens of parks and nature reserves covering a total of around 1,000 acres.

Lunchtime at Bermuda High School, Hamilton.

The announcement of an award at the Dog Show
inspires a spontaneous response from
Diane Adams and Buck.

Spanish Point. You are never too young to learn.

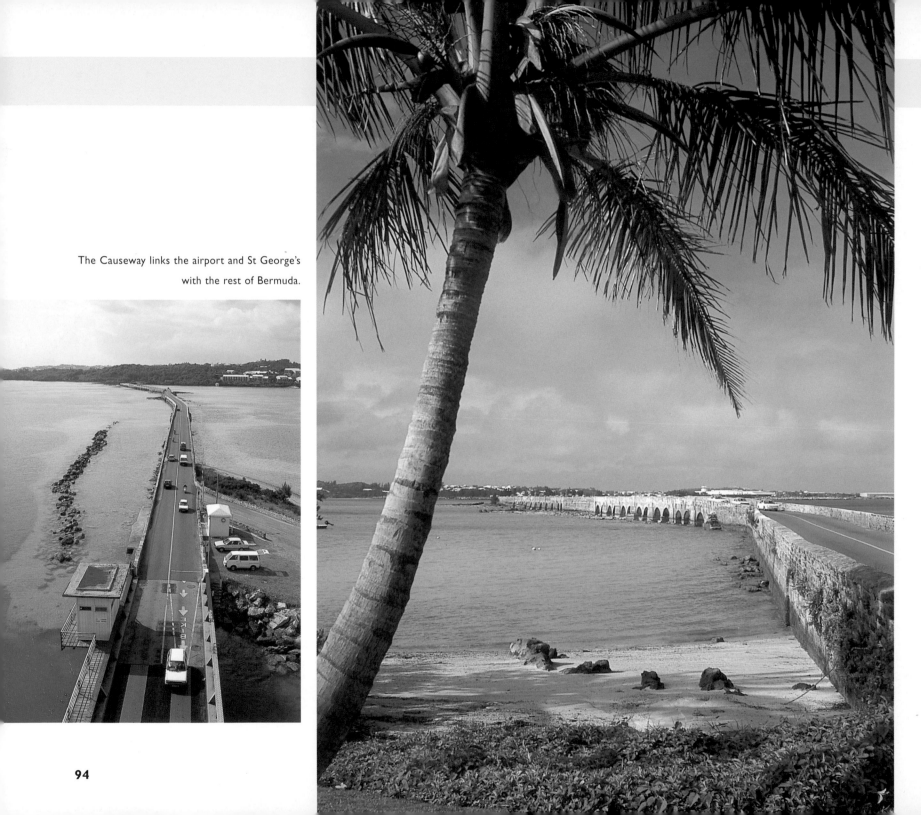

The Causeway links the airport and St George's with the rest of Bermuda.

The ambitious Bermuda Railway was inaugurated in 1931, but then dismantled in 1947 – the year after cars were legalised in Bermuda. Today the Railway Trail provides a safe, quiet right of way for horse riding, walking and cycling along most of the route.

The unfinished church on Church Folly Lane in St George's was begun in the late nineteenth century, when St Peter's showed serious signs of wear. Unfortunately, half the congregation steadfastly refused to move from St Peter's. The protracted debate was never resolved, and the unfinished church remains unfinished even after the National Trust completed its restoration.

Following a Remembrance Day service, the congregation wait for the march passed outside St Peter's in St George's.
The church began as a temporary building in 1612, then was converted into a permanent structure in 1619. The building
was also used for parliamentary meetings until the Old State House (then Sessions House) was built in 1620.

In 1609 Admiral Sir George Somers led a second group of settlers bound for Jamestown, Virginia. On July 28th a violent storm wrecked his flagship – *Sea Venture* – on the reef to the east of Bermuda. Just as Shakespeare's *Tempest* took no lives, all 150 people survived. Somers built two escape vessels out of salvaged materials and local cedar, then continued to Virginia. A replica of *Deliverance* – one of Somers' ships – stands on Ordnance Island.

Remembrance Day in King's Square, St George's. The original capital of Bermuda was founded in 1612. The town hall is a restored eighteenth century building.

One of Bermuda's three independent banks.

The Crystal Caves were discovered in 1907 by boys searching for their cricket ball. A floating pontoon rises and falls 4ft on the tidal waters inside the cave.

The bar at the White Horse in St George's.

Waiting for the rain to clear.

The Swizzle Inn, Blue Hole Hill, Hamilton
Parish, is the island's oldest pub and restaurant,
and is famous for its Rum Swizzle.

St David's lighthouse, to the east of the airport
runway, stands above one of Bermuda's most
isolated communities.

A Martello tower overlooks Whale Bone Bay on St George's Island.

In the nineteenth century Fort St Catherine in St George's Parish replaced a wooden fort built in 1614 above
the beach where the survivors of the *Sea Venture* came ashore.

The Mid-Ocean Club is the hub of social life for the exclusive residential area of Tucker's Town. Its private beach is adjacent to the Natural Arches (far right).

The Bermuda Biological Station overlooking Ferry Reach is a research and education centre specialising in marine studies.

Tobacco Bay is a tranquil lagoon half a mile west of Fort St Catherine.

Governor Thorold Masefield inspects the
Bermuda Regiment in front of the Cenotaph in
Hamilton at the opening of Parliament.

POMP AND PAGEANTRY

The Regimental Band marches passed the Premier, Pamela Gordon (in pink), outside the Cabinet Building then along Front Street.

Pomp and pageantry

The Union Jack flag is raised outside the
Cabinet Building.

The Bermuda Regiment outside the Cabinet Building.

The first sighting of the Longtails or White-tailed tropic birds (*Phaethon lepturus*) heralds the coming of summer. After a winter feeding on fish and squid in the Atlantic, they arrive in Bermuda to mate, nest and rear young from March to October. They nest in small holes in the cliffs, though this sculpture sits on the eastern boundary of the city of Hamilton.

Dave Saunders has been a freelance photographer and writer for 20 years. His work has been published in a wide variety of international publications. He is author of a dozen books on travel, photography, advertising and scuba diving, including HIGHLIGHT JAMAICA, also published by Macmillan.

Photograph by John Saunders

ACKNOWLEDGEMENTS

My thanks go to all those who helped and inspired me
during the preparation of this book, especially:

Diane Adams (& Buck), Eugene Ball, Johnny Barnes,
Phil Bayliss, Hal Browne, Michael Butt,
Bill & Rosanne Cox, John Cox, Nicholas Dill,
David Dodwell, Stevie Dread, Brian Duperreault,
Fed Fernandez, Wolfgang Greiner, Chris Heslop,
Wendy Davis Johnson, Steven Jones, Jimmy Keys,
Eleanor Kingsbury, Arthur Lugo, June & Arthur Morris,
Graham O'Connell, Gordon Price, Jo Roberts,
Scott Stallard, Joy Sticca, Mike Toynbee,
Charles Webbe, Jane Whigham, Mike & Diana Winfield